Gallery Books
Editor Peter Fallon

SHALLOW SEAS

Justin Quinn

SHALLOW SEAS

Gallery Books

Shallow Seas
is first published
simultaneously in paperback
and in a clothbound edition
on 17 September 2020.

The Gallery Press
Loughcrew
Oldcastle
County Meath
Ireland

www.gallerypress.com

ISBN 978 1 91133 795 9 *paperback*
       978 1 91133 796 6 *clothbound*

A CIP catalogue record for this book
is available from the British Library.

Shallow Seas receives financial assistance
from the Arts Council.

Contents

for Tereza

Platform

1

First to settle. Hallstatt culture.
The people on this table hill
left bits and bones that turned to mulch or
gravel after a while.

Now leaves drift down the slope and catch
upon a corpse that's losing heat,
the flesh relaxed as on a couch
into this stretch of soil and concrete.

A few hours back this man was part
of all the city's noise and colour,
in CC shots the flipped-up collar,

involved with others, it appeared,
amidst the neon and day-glo —
bright edge of those dark shelves of clay.

2

Accountants, teachers, mobsters —
the people on this table hill
are walking labradors or lobsters
across the meadow, close at heel.

The shallow Cenomanian sea
sweeps back and forth above their heads.
The currents or the woodlands sigh
and sway and swirl beneath blue heights

that in the end are purely skies.
Here are some other of the eye's
brief misadventures:

the shoals are clouds, the wrack is rust,
and those fleet lobsters just
relaxed Zwergpinschers.

3

Circling the hill, the only vultures
are property developers —
the bits and bones that turn to mulch or
mud put money in their purse.

The orchards, mills and farmsteads
go under tides of concrete, brick
and tarmac as the city spreads,
this platform left out of the uptick.

And in the future rooms the ghosts
gaze out on plots of shrubs and trees
cut back by unit costs,

hovering there hour after hour —
white noise — an ever lower trace
the fewer leaves there are.

4

These have come to rest in sand:
some trilobites, perhaps a whale,

shellfish. And then turn into land.
Mud after a while

when homelessness makes people scrape
and scrape some rooms out of the stone.
The mother cooks some grains, a scrap
of meat and water. The father's down

in the village still. A low cough.
Outside there's rain and high winds sweep
through oak and beech — they groan and sigh.

Further back inside the cave
a child has drifted off to sleep
on a seabed of a long, lost sea.

5

Above this table hill, the sky
is crossed by contrails, fast and loose —
the flights to New York, Beijing, Moscow
as near to free as peace allows.

The leaves drift down the slope and catch
on gun emplacements, chainlink wire
and signs that went up on this patch
two decades into the Cold War.

Now that the warring odds were evened
the earth and sky had no suggestions
for those long years of non-event.

And nothing happened here. Which threw
everyone back on two old questions —
How to live? What to do?

6

Meanwhile for two millennia
the casual sound of crockery
being readied for a meal down many a
path or road; meanwhile the rockery

of Cambrian gods turning to grain.
Meanwhile the corpse is losing heat.
Meanwhile the chickweed white and green.
Meanwhile the springtails on their beat.

I'm running laps or walking round
the table hill's perimeter.
A thousand years is telescoped

in seconds. Power rises and is ruined.
It leaves its signs in sandy matter.
And meanwhile fossils have escaped.

7

We're walking through the sandy woods.
We're climbing up to the plateau.
There's wheat with hardly any weeds,
the grain going in and out of shadow.

We lie down in some flowers — pure kitsch
we can't resist — just for a blast —
our flesh relaxed as on a couch,
our circuits wholly earthed at last

and our heads blown open by the song
that's coming loud and good
up through the ground until it's ours,

and anyway weren't we just saying
this is how we should
see out the next few million years?

8

The forest comes into its own
at night. Darkness in the trees,
drawn up by roots from clay and stone,
spills through the sky like oil through seas.

I'm straying through the aeons. The path
went quickly from beneath my feet
into wood shadow. Ghosts catch my breath
along this stretch of soil and concrete —

some older, some younger. For hours
they whisper like the leaves
their tales of overlapping lives.

I'm lost in them, too far, too late,
and not until first light
I know which century is ours . . .

9

and a horse, not a mastodon,
comes wading through the mist
across the tillage in the dawn.
Its rider flicks a wrist

and picking up the pace it turns
through a patch of burdock and wild rhubarb
and ghosts of Cenomanian ferns.
Beyond, in swathes of smog, the suburbs.

A few eras back this horse was part
of wilderness and its force poured
past trees like a wave through shallow seas.

The rider's talking softly to it.
It's talking back. They both intuit
what the other almost says.

10

The signs, abstracted from the land,
make languages across the earth.
They are like plastics pressed in sand
or clay, slow-bleached, an afterbirth

of business projects and sacred songs —
the scattered waste of puckered bottles
and bags, unbroken by the throngs
of hyphae, nematodes and beetles.

But even these are natural too —
all the city's noise and colour,
its signs and screens that speed us through

with no be at the end of seem.
And though the roots and spores are duller
and slower they hustle all the same.

11

They hustle and they schlep. They reach
out for the minerals and sugars.
They harbour dreams of getting rich
like moguls or determined showgirls.

They sing in wind! They scintillate
in ice! These trees part of the chatter
that fills the forest early and late —
say 'hi!' or 'more!' or 'what's the matter?' —

that our talk's part of too. And this,
come from a man who met his killer,
in CC shots the flipped-up collar.

I frame the shot so I don't miss
his shade. I'm looking at my phone.
It's looking back and says we're fine.

12

For these trees at the plateau's edge
a human life must seem as long

as a mayfly's is to us; old age
comes briefly after birth. They blink.

Our talk a rush of complex beats,
then silence, flesh drained in the ground.
And for the ghosts of trilobites
Hallstatt to now's a flicker — sound

of running, sights of sheets of ice
advancing and then petering out.
Then, as the dawn's mist cleared,

involved with others, they appeared,
the megafauna, strolling about,
gazing through the aeons at us.

13

Meanwhile the corpse has cooled. Police
have come and gone. A judge has parsed
the killer's plea for his release,
and over the long sweep of karst,

their centuries reduced to gist,
mulched and flattened in a heap,
then flattened further till they're just
the lightest leaf print layered deep,

are towers and factories, a fence that juts
more into forest with the years,
meanders of the rush-hour cars,

the smog in skeins above their flow,
are twists of neon and day-glo,
sky-mazes of commercial jets.

14

I'm running laps. The sun has risen
beyond the plateau's edge. These oaks
stand black against the red horizon.
My legs are hurting. My chest aches.

I'm running laps around the hill.
The pheasants stalk the undergrowth.
I heave in air and then exhale.
Out of my mouth, wraith after wraith.

The pheasants, whales and mastodons,
the lobsters as they move and love,
Zwergpinschers as they sniff Great Danes,

and horses, too, take in the day,
pulsing, watching, a while alive,
bright edges of those dark shelves of clay.

Heart Song

I see the deer long after it sees me —
kept breathing by inhibitors and fibrates
beyond my natural span. Both our pulse rates
ramp up round now. I'll bet that he or she

is reckoning I might stop its heart with lead,
surviving even longer on its flesh.
I'll bet my presence is enough to flush
it to the woods with something much like dread.

But for a while we're here. Stock-still. Alone,
except for swarms of polyphonic insects.
It lays down beats to do with dying and sex,
beats I can't hear (I only hear my own).

We've got no lyrics yet, although the song
is old as our two species — and do we need
some new ones now. So it gives the nod
(kind of) before it flings itself headlong

into the piny shadows, startling birds.
The forest murmurs something now and again.
I take my pills years after it has gone
and hang around here trying to catch the words.

Eight Radioactive Tableaux (with Venus and Adonis)

There are no clouds. Thunder out of nowhere.
The boar herd at a gallop through the woods.
Haunch to haunch twisting through the brush and weeds
like shoals through seas, like starlings through the air.

A little fazed by people, they steer clear
of Sunday trippers, seeking out deep shades —
the forest still uncut by backhoe spades.
Like shy actors in the tabloids' glare.

❖

Fig. 2. There are few trees across the plain,
but undergrowth is tall and old and thick.
Small creatures weave through it, the larger trick
the hunt by holding still where they have lain.

He's come here to a halt, hot on the spoor.
Eye-glint in the brush. Flecked and ruddied
flank behind brown leaves. He has just readied
his stance. He has just raised the point of his spear.

❖

Irradiated flesh. They love the ground.
Their snouts sift through its microscopic germs,
searching for tubers, roots, bulbs and earthworms.
They love the acorns and the nuts strewn round.

Rainstorms turning the floor to splash and spill.
Or days-long drizzle seeping slowly down
into the earth. Or snowfall by the ton.
From clouds that drifted here from Chernobyl.

❖

He misses and the tusk unzips his thigh.
An inch or two over, he would have killed it.
The ground and trees are suddenly, wildly tilted.
Caught in their sickening twist, he knows he'll die.

Boar: as though its stench, rank and fierce,
is pressing into him and leaves no room
for even breath. All of the forest's gloom
come to a point in its blunt, bristling force.

❖

It looks like urban wasteland anywhere:
the sunlight flooding through the damaged ceilings;
where there were cars and people, now there's silence;
living rooms and shop floors are open air.

But this is all fenced off. A military post,
well-staffed, stands at the entrance to the Zone.
For all the books and studies, it's not known
whether they guard the future or the past.

❖

Now his lover is arriving, first
of all the others. His eyes are turning dim.
The life is suddenly rushing out of him —
flustered, detailed — surging through the forest

into the sky. A cataclysmic moan
is coming from her body like a wave
that wants to seize him from the new-made grave.
(She is a god, whatever that might mean.)

❖

The catfish in the cooling pond have grown
to monstrous lengths as they've no predators.
The boars graze brazenly — not even tours
can faze them in the 30 Kilometre Zone.

Safety procedures are more finely grained
across the world, signed off by ministers.
Fig. 7. There are yellow canisters
bricked up 500 metres in the ground.

❖

She is raising her arms. She is begging
the very ground to break itself in two.
She is screaming at the other gods: undo
this death. Undo this death. She is wrecking

and ripping up the oak, the pine and olive.
Now she's staring at the lichen and the moss.
Now she's staring at the aphids and the mice.
She is wondering why any of these are alive.

Street Weeds

YARROW, OR SOLDIER'S WOUND WORT

The skin is raked and torn
by thistle and by thorn,
and war makes bodies bleed —
belovèd women, men.
Long back they used this weed
for wounds, time and again.
And here it still waits for
the rumours of new war.

BARLEY GRASS

Outwaiting definitions.
Weed/nonweed. Or wishing/
not wishing to escape
our apartment block,
or my body's shape.
That danger. Air to rock.
Genus grades to genus.
First, the others, then us.

MUGWORT

Where do roads go?
This weed can't know
or will not say,
dark-leaved, chest-high,
along the way.
The world flows by.
Will this weed go?
It's swayed, but no.

TIMOTHY

I landed earlier today.
Are you able to say
which grass it is? Can you
translate this street for me?
The wars, the heroes, too?
No, my flight's not leaving
later in the evening.

HEDGE MUSTARD

Skeleton of air.
Ugly, bleak and bare.
Long stems unleaved. Buds
stay buds though it's old.
Like small yellow studs.
Says it must withhold
self from the broken world,
petals packed and furled.

FESCUE

On every continent, fescue
stands tall (and by our bus-stop too).
It moves with all the other weeds
in winds, and nods, *oh yes, oh yes,*
wondering how it might get its seeds
up to the moon. With such finesse
it's won the world, and now, on cue,
its pollen coats a spaceman's shoe.

TANSY

Two sisters loved this flower
while their own love turned sour,
and neither ever knew
this was the other's favoured bloom.
One died, the other too.
Their daughters then met in a room
and found the tansy flower
had bitter and sweet power.

RYE GRASS

The street's co-ops amass
their detailed minutes. Grass
like this grows all the same.
That the house recognize
this vegetation by its name.
That the house employ its eyes
and get this grass's thisness
in Any Other Business.

CHICORY

Exploding from a pavement's crack,
these plants are nature pushing back.
With nothing but the smallest sleight
the shoots slide round the concrete pours
and muscle their way to the light.
Then flowers break out in scores and scores,
saying: 'The earth is done with you.
The future is our shade of blue.'

PLANTAIN

A leaf of vernal leather.
Hard to make out whether
it waits ahead of feet
or burgeons in their wake.
A man walks down the street,
long coat, a wide-awake.
Is this before or after?
Is there crying or laughter?

CHICKWEED

Can it be greed
that drives chickweed?
Its stems invade
the earth we tend.
Or is it afraid
that we will send
all green to seed
for our great need?

DANDELION

Sun on the ground
lounges around.
Through with the sky,
at least today,
it wants to try
this cracked driveway,
this old playground,
this fresh grave mound.

CANNABIS

Roots crack the concrete surface in slo-mo.
And all the rowdy weeds begin to grow.
Down to the last muscle, tendon and sinew
I have relaxed at last. Look at the sky!
I can't remember it being quite so blue.
The whole long awful winter not once high.
Lounging outside our building, I smile and greet
the evening clouds arriving on our street.

Child of Prague

O little man, imperial gewgaw, I say
you're awesome! Millions come from everywhere to see
you lounging laid-back on an altar here in Prague
as gilded plaster rays explode in spears behind you —
incendiary device that's been going off, mind you,
for centuries now. O small man, drop the humble brag,

you're awesome! You've got such badass boogie shoes!
Daily you put on matinées and evening shows
to teach the generations love and love and love
(if they could only learn the moves). You shuffle there
so fast beneath your sequined skirt and with such flair
that we can't see it, though we know nothing in the Louvre

comes close to your sweet sculpted beauty. You're divine!
Two fingers raised, you hold your right hand in a sign
suggesting calmly there's no doubt at all we'll win,
not Churchill's victory (your fingers are laid flush),
but one that makes a world war seem a bang and flash.
You're telling us, 'Stay cool. You're good. I've got this one.'

And in your left hand rests a *globus cruciger* —
the world, a cross on top for keeping it secure.
To you it's lighter than a toddler's beach ball.
You roll it slightly and tides swing through the seven seas.
You tilt it now and then with grand seigneurial ease
to give the climate-change deniers a wake-up call.

The *putti* love you. They're going nuts around the peace
that your small wooden body keeps there in its pose.
Their skin is silver paint. They mime a Come-All-Ye.
The church's baroque orders, arches, architraves,
its volutes rippling seismically across the nave's
oh-slow-paced space, all this is coming out from YOU

(all caps), from YOU! The church agrees that you are awesome,
so much so that the nuns must drink a lot of Assam
to brace themselves to work each day in your fierce presence.
They lay wide leas of flowers about your tiny feet
and sing the happiest hosannas. They gently fight
back tourist crowds who have more apps than sense.

Look at you! Cooking up miracles to beat the band.
The doctors dance about, saying they can't understand.
You don't hang round for the applause, your boogie shoes
are moving quicker than the videos upload.
O far-out Child of Prague, O lovely cross-dressed lad,
you're five hundred years old and still you're breaking news!

They love you most of all in Ireland. There you chill
across the country on every second farmhouse sill.
The night before a wedding, they take you out-of-doors
and place you underneath a tree to watch the weather.
And there you are, all comfy, nestled in the heather —
with you on guard, no rain approaches, no cloud dares.

Then there's my aunt in Bray, sitting in the sun-room.
Last time I saw her she asked me to write this poem,
and here we are. (Hi Lorna! How's this going so far?
A bit long, isn't it? I'll soon be winding up.
There's some who'll say I'm nothing but a cheeky pup,
but you'll know it's all fun, which sometimes poems are for.)

Perhaps the clinching proof you're awesome, little man,
beyond the grandstand miracles, is that you can
bring laughs to Lorna when my efforts flag.
She loves you too. She's asked me if I'll send her medals
that picture you with *putti*, wreathes and votive petals,
and this poem too. Please take them to her, Child of Prague.

Jerome

Like CIA people who
        really thought that the
USA grew
        directly from the roots of, eh,
Greece and Rome, and so set about the work
        of civilization
(think: you arrive in a country with some fact sheets,
        instructions you don't fully follow

and, let's say, three hundred words
        of the language, or
one of the herds
        of dialect that graze there for
no reason you can see — *you* bring reason,
        Roman pillars, empire,
and when you depart the country some months later
        you leave it marshalled, oh, marching towards

the geo-political
        strategy du jour —
savannahs crawl
        with lions, tigers and bears who're
sipping martinis, intrigued by poems
        in the latest *New Yorker*
and pondering whether or not James Bryant Conant
        didn't overdo it after all;

in fairness bravely dying
        sometimes when a bear
or lion's not buying
        the gin, the poem, the proffered chair),
some people swagger round the place with good
        insurance, quite the cis,
certain that their dreams, their junk, their undergarments
        and their apparel all line up, hying

like good ducks across Fresh Pond;
        and here they are,
    sashaying around
        the pillars of the Widener
as though propelled by universal truth
        (copyright: them, or their
alma mater, which they will later say is them,
        closing the crest's books with a laser wand).

    Others, fortunately, don't.
        And if they sashay
    it's not a front
        for secret funding or a play
in some over-complex shadow game. They know
        the further folds, fractals
and necessary parti-coloured fripperies
        of reasoning; they know that, to be blunt,

    lions are misunderstood:
        though fearsome and grand
    most lions would
        like you to speak their language and
will be patient with you as you learn it.
        They watch you as you're trans-
lated, clearly amused by how you've lost yourself
        in versions, the original gone for good.

    Your true self, maybe, was born
        centuries ago
    in Cyrene, torn
        from there or happy to go
to end your days in Alexandria
        in its great library —
vast, cavernous stacks, arcades that shade the pages
        full of symbols opening to the foreign.

Or your true self sat at a
        table, robes *plus belles*
than, say, Zsa Zsa
        Gabor's in a swords-and-sandals
'50s flick, your leg brushed by the gold mane
        of your lion friend who
— what else? — line edits how you take the holy word
        and version it, so that the original

        's no longer needed by
        Bible Belt preachers
who rarely try
        to talk to lions, or teachers
of religion in Irish primary schools
        who only spare the rod
because the law says so, and *really* think the truth's
        theirs to print on a child's palm or thigh.

        Different empires, same justice,
        or lack thereof.
But, tell me this,
        where else might we meet with a prof-
essor who is just, who will see this text's
        unfairnesses as quick
as airport security would spot a few tanks
        packed neatly in my carry-on — 'Sir, is

        this your bag?' — I might have known —
        but in the empire's
green training zone,
        alive to beauty and inspires
alertness to the play of politics?
        A place where the language
is important — Greek or Czech or even English —
        where lions lounge temporarily in stone.

Elegy for a Werewolf

i.m. Ivan Martin Jirous

I can't believe the stylish, unbowed swagger
with which you passed through prisons in the '80s.
      Marched round and slapped and hurled
about your cell, none of it troubled the great ease
you ranged in brazen rhyme over the world.

A kind of roughneck dandy, like Mick Jagger
howling in Hyde Park in 1969,
      you flounced about the place.
But then went on your knees and made the sign
of the cross, in prayer, asking God for grace.

Then revolution. Freedom. The drunken stagger
of your late poems pointlessly down the page.
      You'd sometimes flash your dick
in bars (which you thought wit), and strip on stage.
Jail kept your talent disciplined and quick.

But you were never going to play the makar
to your friend Havel in the Castle. Stalked
      in those years by a shade,
a werewolf in your lines who scared and mocked
and drew you towards him, you saw the life you'd made.

Nickname: Crazy Asshole. (In Czech *Magor*.)
Calling: poet, saint, felon, misfit.
      Rest easy underground,
who never rested easy over it.
Your rhymes sing clearer: death turned up the sound.

Hannah Wilke's Armpit Hair

Here's Hannah Wilke's armpit hair.
Observe its two black patches' boast —
Playboy-model stance — that grossed
I'd say a little change for her

but grossed out gazes, men like me
who sit there gawping in a row.
Pink and plucked, a little raw,
is what they thought they'd paid to see.

Instead they get the jettish tangles,
tang of salt, the strands unsmooth,
hairy beastie peepshow booth,
feminist working the man-angles

with stick-on scars of bubble gum
placed on her torso, soliciting
their want, 'You like? Is this your thing?
These stuck-up lips, they make you come?'

The same eyes stare out of the wreck
that cancer made of her sweet body,
full frontal, seated, all her beauty
now in the eyes that still would deck

a man for flinching where he'd lusted
oh once-upon-a-time. O tell me,
Hannah Wilke, brunette bombshell me —
for your clear SOS has lasted —

show us again the strands so loved,
before they turn to artshop lore.
O fuck with all our heads once more,
and tell us of the art you lived.

Oak Song

Springtails churn through the clay around my toes,
the worms as well. These laddies bring a breeze
down to the chilly depths that my legs squeeze
so I stay upright no matter how it blows.

I've been around for, oh, don't ask how long.
I die as well, but first I'll see off you
and your whole culture's pumped-up POV.
Nothing personal. Cheer up. Here's some birdsong.

I take my time. I range out languidly
and say about a syllable a year.
Can you imagine that? To your quick ear
this is just leaf noise in the canopy.

There was a guy once. Saved me from an axe.
I told him I'd do anything in thanks.
And he said, anything? brushing my flanks.
Well, that was fun. I told him to relax,

but OK, yes. I'd let him know soon when.
I could feel the sugars moving through my phloem.
In a few days I was ready to show him
just how completely sprites lay mortal men.

But he's like, can we do this later? Dude,
it's you who does the waiting, not this nymph.
There was a little blood, a little lymph,
when I served him to boar as finger food.

So I refolded myself in the oak,
and felt my limbs like syrup slowing down.
I soon was hazy about just what I'd done,
and centuries went drifting by like smoke.

Down in the roots, the vessels, tubes and coils
of microscopic life are effervescent;
beside them, carbon trades brisk and incessant.
It's hard to say what's mine and what the soil's

as fungal filaments have long ago
finagled their way into my great roots,
and I'm plugged in their network — the set-up suits
us all, small frissons in the sylvan flow.

Stories, sex: they don't apply to me,
not any more. Perhaps they never did.
The grid beyond the mycorrhizal grid
is vaster, older, like necessity.

There are no stories: there is a green height
and black earth. Between these, only processes.
Trees stand around the place oblivious.
To you at least. They're busy. They eat light.

Forest Songs

I walk into the woods
for nothingness, for rest.
But pulling on what rots
the sugars of the forest
go racing from the roots.

I walk into the woods.
Beneath the canopy
there's chaos. It's all wrong.
Birds sing obliviously
to every other song.

I walk into the woods
beyond the bigbox stores.
There's old upholstery placed
for sleeping under stars
near the dumpster waste.

I walk into the woods
and deer freeze where they stand.
I freeze as well and stare
like I'm all zen or stoned,
like I'm not even there.

I walk into the woods
like going into a church,
but find a serpent there,
boar ambling through the birch,
and flies thronging the air.

I walk into the woods
and see, for syrup's sake,
the aphids overdo it.
Then, mouth to ass, ants suck
the sugar aphids shit.

I walk into the woods
300 million years
back: ferns, colossal, rule.
And this whole tract secures
three cents of fossil fuel.

I walk into the woods
and cut birch to its pith.
Through winter I'll clean soot
and woodstove glass streaked with
black tears of creosote.

I walk into the woods
and come out with a fever
that boils my brain, tick-borne,
as much chance to recover
as Chidiock Tichborne.

I walk into the woods
with my young son and show him
how sapwood is yay wide,
how xylem and how phloem
then die into heartwood.

I walk into the woods.
Like plastic in leaf litter
still looking at my phone's
enthralling splash and glitter,
annoying eco fauns.

I walk into the woods.
Very soon I've strayed.
Going on now fifty winters.
So many trees destroyed.
My hands are full of splinters.

I walk into the woods.
I'm better by the hour.
Not much light inside,
but herbs send through the air
oh waves of phytoncide.

I walk into the woods,
the blossoms spreading wider —
larkspur, buttercup.
Everywhere the water
in gallons going up.

Regreen

Green comes even so
from cracked concrete, bare
black branches. The doe
rocks to the roe-deer.
Pollen everywhere,
on me, even here,

as I walk past the fields, along the road.

Summer's coming in,
is the track I sing.
Inside a dark inn
the girl who brings my beer
has lots of the spring
in her, oh, even here.

Then I walk towards the fields, along the road.

There are people packed
like leaves through the ground
in each plot and tract,
dozing, year on year,
tossing and turning round
gently — even here

where I walk past the fields, along the road.

These ones sing their airs
from lodgings in the earth,
asking me, who cares,
and who'd like to hear
what they've left of mirth
even now and here,

when I walk past the fields, along the road.

I will rot like wood
no matter how I flee.
Still, the day is good.
Old songs learnt by ear
make free, oh, make free
with me — even here

as I walk past the fields, along the road.

Skøg Urban Hub Elegy

i.m. Ivan Blatný

While outside spring is warming up the land
you're sitting here with me in this café,
a little chilly, as you've slept in clay
so long, a little tremor in the hand,

but otherwise you're fine as you take in
the place you left some eighty years ago.
There isn't much new stuff for you to know.
Mainly the ghosts will wonder how you've been,

orphaned so young and raised by your grandmother,
then orphaned by your home town when you left
for England, forever afterwards bereft —
one day your country turned into another.

Meanwhile the spring is waking up the weeds
in pavement cracks and cobbles on the square
of nineteenth-century apartment buildings where
you lived; it's waking up at different speeds

the flowers and leaves of alder, birch and ash
along the city's rail embankments; waking
green from the ground beside gasholders' flaking
paint and gorgeous rust: a flame, a flash

that sets the place alight. Winter's done for,
and heat brings looseness to the limbs around us.
Let's order now: the inked waiter has found us
like two Braun statues on a factory floor.

The post-industrial café's filled with the young
in one another's arms, offline or on.

Welcome back to all this! While you were gone
it more or less continued, but unsung

so well as you sang it. What have the years
left of you here? Or left of anyone?
Let's go and see. Here's Brno in the sun —
the city's full of hints and souvenirs.

We'll borrow skateboards, see if we can't find
the old addresses by the new signposts
and stop for tea with both your parents' ghosts:
they'll cry and hug you, a child so shy and kind.

Island Sonnet

My island month is over and I go back.
I wrote. Was lonely. I saw the other islands
locked in the lake on days of sunny silence.
At night, I read a long meandering book.

Deer and boar would make the odd foray
across the frozen fields. I settled in
and found a way to stretch out on my own.
The month is over. Soon I'll get the ferry.

And I go back to you, my only love,
in the midst of it the whole while I was gone,
the hassle I can't hack now and again

and need to see reduced to just a fleck,
a flake that falls somewhere over the lake.
But now you draw me. You are why I leave.

A Cappuccino for Robert Cremins

They are all still there. Say, 1988.
They pop out to Blackrock or Cornelscourt.
They are large in their world. The shopping cart
fills up with candy of mythic size and weight.

They are not weak. They can hear everything.
Pishogues still linger in their memory
and they do not quite believe technology.
Beneath their accent, different brogues still sing.

They are all clearly still there. Babies in prams
are not yet criminals or ministers
or both. On Sundays they say paternosters
and even married sex brings with it qualms.

We're twenty, but they have power: what they say
goes to show, oh, what we've long forgotten.
We can't shrink them just yet to Buster Keaton.
They suffer, but in ways that we can't see.

In all of Ireland there's only one café
that can make cappuccino. South Anne St.
Perhaps we sit there talking three hours straight,
still yet to cry and cry for these one day.

Elegy with Java Chip Frappé

I was standing on the corner of Stroupežnický St, my back to the synagogue, looking at a tree full of all the dust of August, and past the tree to the crossroads at Angel, and past the crossroads to Plzeň St, and past Plzeň St to Palacký Bridge. The evening was still a long way off, the sun was scorching my back and the hot air shimmered everywhere. In my pocket I had a pile of cash for working overtime on Soviet hopper cars.

— Jan Zábrana, 'A Pile of Cash'

I'm watching you from Starbucks across the street.
You've got a pile of cash and you seem happy.
Who would have thought a Java Chip frappé
would lie there hoving in the narrow strait,

the street that's only seventy years wide
that lies between us? Trams glide past as well
like alternating current, stopping a while
to make crowds surge and ebb on either side.

English, Russian: you spent your life between them.
'I'll die in falsified history,' you said.
My friend, where else is there to die? The dead
stack best in fake news or a national anthem.

The Java Chip frappé still in my hand,
I leave and follow you across the river
where there's a dreadful shithole you revere,
a kind of pub plus brothel, hotdog stand,

flophouse and rowdy tearoom all in one.
You're happy still and there's that pile of cash
still in your pocket. The last of the sunrays flash
across the river. Now for the night's fun.

Wagon-Lit Nižbor

1

When we were stopped in Lviv we needed air
and pulled the window down a bit.
A blade of bitter cold slid in; with it
a voice, an old man's voice: 'The children here...'
He paused to catch his breath a moment, 'They...'
But we were off. For hours then all we saw
were fields and fields of luminescent snow.
And we heard nothing further till the day.

2

From Ústí up to Dresden, in the night,
what seemed like crowds moved up and down the train,
their shuffling syncopated with the din
the wheels made on the rails. From left to right
the carriages tilted into every slope
along the Elbe's twisting corridor.
Once someone tried the handle of our door,
thought better of it and we went back to sleep.

3

Towards evening the train came to a sudden stop
outside a village called Lesnoye. Silence.
Nothing stirring in the wooded highlands.
The houses and the buildings of the co-op
stock-still — or rather they warped and rusted and tore
at speeds so low their change escaped the eye.
Then we were off — the forest slipping by,
the dwellings moving normally once more.

4

There was the time a child joined us a while.
Perhaps he'd lost his parents on the road.
Someone had lifted him out of the crowd
at Košice main station not a mile
behind (we'd seen most of those goings-on,
on the platform hundreds trying to board,
but just in time the carriage doors were barred).
We dozed a little. When we woke he was gone.

5

In the Exclusion Zone, with curious ease
we sailed across wild meadows in the streets,
past concrete plains arrayed with fallen struts,
their structures open to the lightest breeze.
We'd heard that some came back in the belief
that they'd be better off where it occurred —
the authorities, it seemed, no longer cared —
like shadows moving through an afterlife.

6

The populations moving, heavily laden.
In Kiev and in Warsaw we saw scores
of people, even children, on the squares
strewn in the way that sheaves in storms lie down.
A sigh gone from each body, they subsided,
gradually nudged and shifted by the stems
of different weeds, and by the ravening teams
of ants and maggots, till their flesh and blood dried out.

7

We pulled the bunks down, spread the sheets across
and passed the bottle back and forth until
the rails rocked us to sleep. We were moving still
when sunlight broke over a field of grass,
a wrecking yard or stretch of silver lake;
and moving still at speed through smaller towns,
the village stations done in creams and browns,
the red-capped station master's drowsy look.

8

We stopped at one called Nižbor towards the evening.
A child spoke to us in the local language.
We gave her sweets. The grass rose to the linkage.
Nearby, at a bar, people were leaving,
loud songs and loud goodbyes. When they were gone,
silence but for a dog's untroubled bark.
The railway tracks stretched off into the dark.
The lights clicked through their signals till the dawn.

Five Odes on a Prague Pub That is Now Called Hostomická Nalévárna

1 CONVERSATION ODE

The ghosts are talking in the walls.
    They're careful to downplay
    exactly what they say,
just adding somewhat to the murmur,
    making the barroom warmer
        with old hearsay.

The ghosts are raging in the walls
    when a lone drinker's here
    having a quiet beer.
They roar and threaten to turn violent.
    Suddenly they'll go silent
        when others appear.

The ghosts are talking in the walls.
    The night is cold outside
    Do they know that they've died?
The barman doesn't catch their order.
    Beyond the wainscot border
        it's cold outside.

2 DISASTER MOVIE ODE

Where else wait it out but here,
everything that is to come?
They have bread and they have beer,
and if needed they have rum.
We will watch the long hand tick —
thirty years will do the trick.

Some days bread will not be fresh.
Shouts will drift in from the street.
Shots perhaps. The surge and thresh
of panicked crowds swept off their feet.
Shutters can be brought down snugly
should events outside turn ugly.

Decades later we'll come out,
eyes unused to light. Mirage:
shapes and colours strewn about,
bits of limbs and fuselage.
We'll pause moments at the door.
Then we'll pick up life once more.

3 INDIGENOUS URBAN ODE

The locals sit around and say
       we aren't local.
        We are pinochle;
    they are mariáš.
      We are cricket; they
are hockey. We're cards; they're cash.

The pub's our local all the same.
       Does that translate?
       Not so great.
      But 'regular' is expressed
     around here in a name
that joins a tree trunk to a guest.

  OK, so maybe each of us
       can then agree
        to be a tree.

Our leaves will fill the gloom
up to the ceiling, *rus*
in urbe — a forest in the room.

4 RURAL ORIGIN ODE

A clearing in the crowds of pine and oak.
A brewery in the hills for centuries.
The kegs are carted down so that townsfolk
can taste what lies beyond the city walls
and dream. In suits or skirts or overalls
they take a seat. They nod. A glass is brought.
    They drift off while the whole world stalls,
        long minutes lost in thought.

A brewery in the hills for centuries.
A clearing in the crowds of pine and oak.
For twenty solid years there'd been no peace.
The villagers were largely unconcerned.
But in the year of '39 they learned
the enemy was near: the Swedish host
    came sweeping in and briskly turned
        the village to a ghost

which rose again when war had petered out
in that same spot, beneath the mountain range,
the forest's shadow stretching miles about.
The village's name as it was before,
which means 'the stranger's place' — though local lore
won't say if he came from the east or west.
    Which means they might still hold the door
        to welcome the new guest.

5 INVITATION ODE

Well, Evan,
I think that heaven
might have some chairs
and battered tables, wares
worn by long use,
the joints a little loose,
so that we'll seem to sway
whenever high winds make their way
into the blithesome crap
we talk. They'll have, say, five good beers on tap.

And Rob,
it's a good job
the old pub's grime
that built up over time
through long regimes
was kept. The wood here gleams
with men and women's lives
gone by — the grain they smoothed survives.
We slide into their stead
along the grooves they made, the stuff they said.

And Paul,
who is on call
beyond Dubai,
you bid us all goodbye
before this bar
reopened. Is it too far
to get here for an evening?
Your thirst that small? Time you were leaving
Al Ain to catch your flight.
We'll raise four glasses in this pub tonight.

Two Sentinels of Plzeň

We keep watch through the day and night
standing on this rooftop height.
We wait. We bode and we abide.
Our gaze remains steady.
The city wakes and works and sleeps
below us. Evening traffic slips
out to tower blocks on green slopes.
We are always ready.

Across the plains, four rivers come.
They find their way here through the hum
of highways, depths of forests, calm
of mountains, spans of leas,
and flow into each other here.
Their waters mix the soils, year
after year, before they steer
as one to northern seas.

They heave ore from the earth. They bring
it here and put it through coke-firing
until it flows out ductile iron —
the furnace halls lit up
all through the night. Arc lights shine
on loading bays and stockyards, a line
of hopper cars bound for the mine,
on chainlink and on scrub.

What powers of air stream through the sky?
We know. When the bombers fly
towards here to knock the town askew,
we are the first to see.
When armies cross the border
we see their movements, see the mortar
flash, then seconds later murder.
Though stoics both, we sigh.

Prowess, loyalty and largesse,
good customs, cleanliness in dress,
we two knights stand for nothing less.
The highest paragons,
five floors above your works and days,
we wait for you to see the skies,
and see us too — the steady gaze,
the resting sword, the stance.

Dresden Therapy Maenad

1

In Dresden, somewhere in the Albertinum
there is a photograph from during the floods
when all the statues stood in one room — plenum
of marble and of plaster whose various muds
were pressed into cool flesh for centuries
and sheltered from the faster flowing moods
outside. Here are the Lares and the Furies,
here is Athena in her different forms,
all turned to fragments and forgotten stories.
And now a person who's been through the firestorms
stands in front of you. What do you feel?
They are cold. They have lost one of their arms.
What's to be done with one more rubble-hill —
try this for size — but make it integral?

2

I feel ripped open. These statues standing here
in twisting drafts of heat have sucked me in
to their events — the lifted hand, the hair
in waves swung by the torso turning on
a plinth — the moments that decide their day.
Suddenly, I feel my body parts begin
to come undone, painfully moving away
on streams of air and water, different speeds
of sediment that settle then like dew.
And here's a Maenad, just as she explodes
with joy, her head thrown up into the void,
her arms and legs blown roughly off. She pleads
for our destruction — that is what she's vowed.
Her marble flesh destroyer and destroyed.

3

This is your father, here in front of you.
There behind him, waiting, is your mother.
There is no furniture. Not much of a view.
Your father steps in closer — there's some bother
in his gaze when he sees you. But she's much quicker
and leaves your prostrate sister and your brother,
twisting her torso round him. Will you attack her?
Or will you take it? The therapist says 'freeze',
the figures turning now a little thicker
as they sag back to their identities.
A rush of wind through leaves, as in the past.
Before the woman removes your mother's face,
see who stands where. What have you realized?
What do you feel? Say it now, at last.

4

What do you feel? Grief. What do you feel?
More grief, in waves, through millions of us,
features twisted freshly red and pale,
a grief no therapy could ever efface,
the bodies laid out on the river meadows,
the burnt limbs cooled by dew. There is no office
that could heal or deal with all these shadows.
They keep on coming in their thousands. They hide
on boats and buses — the widowers, the widows
and the outnumbering orphans all with their dead
close-packed inside them, who mutter, roar
and gnaw the children in the years ahead.
Who are these people milling at the door?
What do they want of us? How many more?

5

Your father and your mother's flesh, like yours,
is made of gravels and alluvials
swirled by the tides and swept to river shores.
We have streamed and slid together. Feeling wells
as we pause looking in each other's eyes,
stock-still, enclosed by heavy sandstone walls,
before we start to move again. Stone lies
in hills of rubble on street after street.
For decades people tried each one for size
against the others to get the courses straight —
their broken bones, their blood, the gradual gain —
until the work was finally complete,
and a great cathedral's rebuilt on the plain,
its every block made integral, again.

Ivana Lomová's Neorealist Portrait
of a Couple

They are sitting at a café table.
Most of the canvas is a hill covered in snow —
its groves bare, the winter river below,
white-dusted roofs, here and there a gable

(Prague's palaces and mills). And on the top
there sits in miniature an Eiffel Tower.
Lustrous greys, as though after a shower.
This says: most of a marriage is backdrop.

The city's laid out in the large vitrine,
an ornament of their long conversation.
And that each of them is from a different nation
could just be further colour in the scene.

They are white, at ease — equals seated,
agreeing and demurring. From Crete to Dover
social democracy ticking over
in rows of concrete buildings centrally heated.

Their children are somewhere. They are not
bivouacking beside a border fence
in the cold, trying not to give offence.
They are not poised to jump a juggernaut.

And they know this. It forms part of their talk.
They change in answer to the change around.
They respond. They turn themselves into background.
After an hour they go out for a walk

along the river, past the ministries,
the offices and big hotels with porters.
They wander through the city's different quarters
and in their pockets they have several keys.

Social Democratic Song

You crowds here on the strand,
great pressure and great heat
have twisted, pulled and strained
the rock below. You meet

and spread yourselves on Sundays,
your shades of flesh revealed
in candy-coloured undies
on this tectonic shield

with fresher gneiss on top.
Its foliations rise
above you, rough outcrop
nearby the criss-crossed rows

of low-rise housing blocks —
beiges, browns and blues,
deck-access doorways, box
by box by box with views

of sky. Grass prints your skin.
Such lovely silicates
have swum for aeons in
the earth to make the state's

social democratic
bedrock. You brush against
each other. Odd erotic
currents gently flensed

by chilly water. Pink cheek
by feldspar jowl. The tons
of generations mean you check
your daughters and your sons.

Adelsö

1

I am lying in a hammock in Sweden,
blue sky beyond a canopy of cherry.
I am resting in a socialistic Eden,
beside long meadows, tall oaks for a king,
sand paths that wander to sweet water, a ring
of road that goes back to the ferry.

This haze and heat might have me half asleep.
The cherry globes bob slightly in the breeze.
The shapes or shades of deer sprint round and leap
through ancient lichened branches; towards the evening
they loudly bell, a sound like awful grieving
about the island's groves and leas.

2

I am lying in a hammock in Sweden,
I might have had a beer or two — beer made
just down the road from here, and brewed to sweeten
such summer days and free this people from
their goodness, their incorruptible aplomb,
for a few hours dreamily swayed.

The label says one Anders Kotz brewed it.
May he do well. He's lifted me on waves
that lift the island also. Feet to the bowsprit,
I'm launched on Lake Malar and headed north.
Frost giants might say what's up with the earth,
if I can find them in their icy caves.

3

The world's on fire this summer: rub two sticks
and miles of forestland will turn to smoke;
the ocean's thermostat went up some clicks
and fish are none too pleased; rain, if rain falls,
runs off the car parks, courts and malls —
the worms ask us is this a joke.

And all the while three brothers in the night,
three corners of the continent, we sigh,
we shout, we argue from the left to right.
Frost giants loose the ice caps from their grip
in the background. And so my crazy trip
up to the north to ask them why.

4

Or am I just asleep? Is this a winding sheet?
My almost cosmic snoring joins the storms
that rough up trees and flatten fields of wheat.
Great currents draw back, mustering their forces.
Out on the lake, waves massing like warhorses.
The hills unfold in flaming forms.

And the wolves run. Is this how the world ends?
Frost giants stood here at the start of things.
The stories tell how two wolves — fierce, immense —
will eat the sun and moon. The sea will rise
and rush across the earth to men's surprise,
the world-tree scorched to its first rings.

5

I am lying in a hammock in Sweden,
between a cherry and a plinth of elm.
Unheard by giants, still alive, world-smitten,
though chill encloses me as light is lost —
a portent or a memory of frost.
Night creatures of the island realm

make noise again: three brothers, belling deer,
a single wolf that's watching from a barrow.
Still uncertain, but if the world's still here
we'll rise and clean up last night's plates and pots,
put dough into the oven, and Anders Kotz
will brew another batch tomorrow.

Earth Options

for Jana Krejzová

Some let it year-long lie.
They can't see its green flame.
If it dies or they die
for them is all the same.

Some shape it into towers
and fill the floors with crowds.
Then money and great powers
accrue. Below them, clouds.

There are many in between.
For instance, who made this cup,
its cindered curves, its sheen
that cedes to ash. Close-up

you see it as a day
quite overcast — cloud and ground
so near your body's clay
that all is safe and sound.

It's made with someone's hands,
their flesh that slipped off bone,
dissolving in wetlands
with leaves and bits of stone,

then brought back to the air,
shaped carefully and fired
to form this earthenware.
Maybe you're lost. Or tired.

Boil water, pour it in.
The cup then gradually curbs

the liquid's splash and spin.
Now take a few dry herbs

and let them fall onto
this lake, close-up a mile
across, astounding you.
Drink it. Breathe a while.

The thing is that our lot
is near superfluous:
the question's rather what
the earth will do with us.

Walk Song

My bag was light,
so I put stones
in it to right
my crooked bones.

The harnessed load
buckled me down,
nose to the road
that led from town —

as though each building,
wall and tree
were now tilting
back against me.

But I was damned
if I'd stop now.
So here I am,
grey hair, wet brow,

through meadows singing
and yet to crack,
a city swinging
off my back.

The Metals

1

The sea is just a mirror of the sky,
some days a sheen and slide of old plate glass,
the tiny currents sifting softly by,
the bladderwrack below stock-still as brass,
and other times not that: strong winds lift peaks
of living water and drop them brusquely down.
Dark forms take shape across the sandy floor.
Two brigs are laden till their timber creaks.
That night a storm comes in. Four hundred drown,
most of them just a few feet from the shore.

2

At Blackrock, Seapoint, Salthill and Dún Laoghaire,
the bodies wash up for a whole weekend,
rocked by the slightest waves, the sea now weary
as its colossal labours reach their end.
Our lives play out along the shore, between
the mountains at our backs and Dublin Bay,
so much left to the will of wind and tide
we have forgotten. Is it a pleasing scene,
a backdrop as we go about our day?
Kneel on the sand and ask these who have died.

3

Dark forms take shape across the sandy floor.
Two piers are built from outsize ashlar blocks,
the granite blown with decades-long furore
out of a hill nearby, the rough-edged rocks
rolled down on rails a mile or two, then dressed

and dropped into the mirrors of the sea,
the courses dry and tight enough to keep
out chaos. Boulevard at last: depressed
or bored or happy, the crowds in safety
take strolls across the salty murderous deep.

4

The years go by in millions, drifting plates
bring scraps of land together, ice sheets melt
and shallow seas race over future states,
which turn to desert, bog or veldt;
this land as well. The waters then draw back
to leave a coast where we'll live for a while.
We shift its rock and sands to suit ourselves
forgetting how the whole thing's turning on a tack
not ours, and not a thing itself, the isle
submerged again in shifting plates and shelves.

5

And we go with it, underneath the waves,
the tiny currents sifting softly by
above the houses, gardens, roads and graves,
above the two great granite arms that lie
engulfed by what they were built to withhold.
The mackerel shoals flaunt argent in the deep,
the ling slip past, and dogfish, solitary,
glide over ashlar flags where we once strolled
and schemed and sighed and stopped to watch the sweep
of cloud and sunset change magnificently.

6

They shift the rock and sands to suit themselves,
these strong-willed nineteenth-century engineers.
They set deep charges in the granite shelves.
They master men and money forty years.
Their names are William Hazeldine, John Rennie,
Netlam Giles, George Smith and Richard Toutcher,
who had the force to face the leeward blast.
They too will find the waves are one too many.
They too will find they failed to hold the future.
The tides will nudge their bones apart at last,

7

who master men and money forty years.
Out of a hill nearby, the rough-edged rocks
come down the metals and form the piers,
pavilions, thoroughfares and ferry docks.
Nearby, the workers make encampments; stench
and filth disturb the upright residents —
'the lowest, and the worst, of human kind'.
The rich are always with us — speaking French,
playing sonatas, applying witty scents —
though finally our flesh will rot, combined.

8

These men grow old, retire and loose their bowels.
They get a few years seated along the front —
pillars of society, mottled jowls,
their pensions crystallized, which leaves the brunt
of crisis to the younger generation.

Conversing on the weather, how it stirs
old memories, small glints of light in dreary
lengths of days, and walking with frustration
as though through storms, here come the pensioners
of Blackrock, Seapoint, Salthill and Dún Laoghaire.

9

The mountains at our backs and Dublin Bay
ahead, we heard their screaming in the night,
after their laden brigs were under way
and ambushed by the storm. We had no light
so there was nothing we could do to help,
but carefully gather them up where we found them
next morning, strewn by the night's events,
their pale and battered bodies draped in kelp
that looked like arms the sea had used to drown them
as proof of its offhand magnificence.

10

The splash of slightest waves, the sea now weary.
The pensioners in armchairs gaze at it,
with cloudy thoughts, their eyesight turning bleary;
in ones and twos, with little fuss, they quit,
while still the wagons trundle down the metals,
while still the waves rush in against the piers,
while still the ferries sail for Holyhead,
while still the tide slips out and sand resettles,
and then flows in. For that the usual tears —
the customary slow increase of the dead.

11

We'll need laments and lullabies at dawn
for these few hundred gone into the ground
to join the shades of generations gone,
compounded and compounded with those drowned
and those who drifted off, life by life,
the voices joining in a choir, which is
the vault and frame of clear parental space.
And in its mist, when storm or shadowed knife
takes people suddenly away like this,
we need a cure of earth, or just this place.

12

The pigweed foaming from the ground, the nettles,
burdocks, chicory and dandelions,
each spring unfold their varicoloured petals,
as well as rhododendron, creeper vines,
viburnum, fuchsia, privets, chestnut trees,
lawns brindled brightly by the buttercup,
and cherry flowers like cloudlets, pink above
the grassy verges. When all of these release
their flakes of light, may they be gathered up
and brought here to this place, set down with love.

13

And my soul magnifies the lovely haze
across the bay on brighter evenings, scud
and distant spinnakers whipping the stays,
all angled to the wind, a rush of blood,
a quickening, a widening of the body's portals,

so it can hold huge festivals, or move
with them outside itself — children's charades
at weekend markets, a dance of particles
through eddying crowds, a drift, a kind of groove,
as well as all our ghosts in gathering shades,

14

And my soul magnifies the shocking days
of spring, unfolding varicoloured petals
out of the black and brown compacted clays,
on Dalkey Hill, eyes following the metals,
observing movements of the sea from land,
which also moves, though its waves are so slow
we call them hills or mountain ranges, lit
by sunlight, straked by rain. We firmly stand
here braced, our breath so brief that soon we go
into the ground and flowers come up from it,

15

from all our ghosts among the gathering shades
as in a stadium, the clicking stiles,
the coastline here to disappear in decades,
the water rushing up our roads, slate tiles
soon dreaming underneath the mackerel shoals
and sailboats on fine days with sea besprent.
If seas are just a mirror of the skies,
the currents and the slipstreams switching roles —
then what great talks are coming, magnificent
palabra of reflections and replies.

16

I mind how we swam on weekend mornings, shocked
when cold saltwater swathed us in itself,
but getting used to it, splashed and rocked,
we struck out further on the sinking shelf.
Brother, father, sister, mother, friends,
we hung down in its deeps, our arms and legs
strumming against the currents after dawn,
the line where grey sky on grey sea depends
beneath our lips, above the sandy dregs.
A seal showed up to ask what's going on,

17

and dropped back in the mirrors of the sea,
that comes and goes in larger flows of space.
Between the offing and the closer lee
we live. Around us, always, currents race,
and gulls drift over. Here we swim, through crowds
of ghosts and of the quick like shoals that play
in moving shades of starlings on a spree
some fathoms down, which are the same as clouds
that idle through the sky above the bay,
or just their shadows on the open sea.

Acknowledgements and Notes

Acknowledgements are due to the editors of the following publications where some of these poems, or versions of them, were published first: *A2, The Artful, Berfrois, BODY, Causeway, The Irish Times, The Manchester Review, The Moth, The New York Review of Books, The New Yorker, Poetry Ireland Review, Poetry Salzburg, Ravt* and *The Yale Review*.

'Regreen' first appeared in *Liberation*, edited by Mark Ludwig (Beacon Press, 2015); it was set to music by Elaine Agnew and was premiered in Prague by the Boston Children's Chorus in July 2015. 'Heart Song' first appeared in *The Hippocrates Book of the Heart*, edited by Wendy French, Michael Hulse and Donald Singer (Hippocrates Press, 2017).

The author gratefully acknowledges a bursary from the Arts Council (Ireland) / An Chomhairle Ealaíon. Also, he wishes to thank Shane and Karin Quinn for the use of their house on an island in a Swedish lake.

Thanks to the following individuals for inspiring, providing help with, or responding to drafts of these poems: Stephanie Burt, Bonnie Costello, Nigel Curtin, Ailbhe Darcy, Selina Guinness, Ernest Hilbert, Cathal McCabe, Alistair Noon, David Quinn, Evan Rail, David Wheatley and Paul Wilson. Heartfelt thanks once again to all the team at Gallery for the care and passion of their work.

> *page* 11   The first sonnet takes some of its moves from Jan Zábrana's 'Dead Girl, Remembered'.
>
> *page* 35   This is inspired by the artist's 'S.O.S. Starification Object Series' (1975).
>
> *page* 36   'Why would a plant care about Mozart?' the late ethnobotanist Tim Plowman would reply when asked about the wonders catalogued in *The Secret Life of Plants*. 'And even if it did, why should that impress us? They can eat light, isn't that enough?' — Michael Pollan, 'The Intelligent Plant', *The New Yorker* (23 and 30 December 2013).
>
> *page* 43   Ivan Blatný (1919-1990) was a Czech poet, born in Brno, who went into exile in the UK in 1948 and spent most of the remainder of his life there in mental asylums.

page 47 The epigraph is the first paragraph of Jan Zábrana's autobiographical story, 'Peklo peněz'.

page 68 I'm indebted to Rob Goodbody's *The Metals: From Dalkey to Dún Laoghaire* (Dún Laoghaire-Rathdown County Council, 2010).